FERGUSON
CAREER BIOGRAPHIES

TWYLA THARP

Dancer and Choreographer

James Robert Parish

Ferguson
An imprint of ☑ Facts On File

Twyla Tharp: Dancer and Choreographer

Ferguson
An imprint of Facts On File, Inc.
132 West 31st Street
New York NY 10001

Library of Congress Cataloging-in-Publication Data

Parish, James Robert.
  Twyla Tharp : dancer and choreographer / James Robert Parish.
      p. cm.
  Includes bibliographical references and index.
  ISBN 0-8160-5828-8 (hc : alk. paper)
  1. Tharp, Twyla. 2. Choreographers—United States—Biography. 3. Dancers—United States—Biography. I. Title.
  GV1785.T43P37 2005
  792.8′2′092—dc22   2004013293

Ferguson books are available at special discounts when purchased in bulk quantities for businesses, associations, institutions, or sales promotions. Please call our Special Sales Department in New York at (212) 967-8800 or (800) 322-8755.

You can find Ferguson on the World Wide Web at http://www.fergpubco.com

Text design by David Strelecky

Pages 95–110 adapted from Ferguson's *Encyclopedia of Careers and Vocational Guidance, Twelfth Edition*

Printed in the United States of America

MP Hermitage 10 9 8 7 6 5 4 3 2 1

This book is printed on acid-free paper.

CONTENTS

1

A WOMAN FOR ALL SEASONS

On October 24, 2002, *Movin' Out* opened on Broadway. The show, which contains no dialogue, features 28 songs by musician Billy Joel and was conceived, staged, and directed by Twyla Tharp, one of the most acclaimed dancers and choreographers the world has known. For her artistic efforts on *Movin' Out*, Twyla received a Tony Award nomination for Director (Musical) and won a Tony Award in the Choreographer category. This huge success was nothing new for Tharp, who is a pioneering talent noted for reaching out in exciting, new, and creative directions.

Tharp arrived on the modern dance scene in the mid-1960s in the wake of such acclaimed 20th-century choreographers as George Balanchine, Merce Cunningham, and Paul Taylor. Within a few years Twyla Tharp was recognized by her peers as a talented visionary. She was hailed as a pioneer of the postmodern dance movement in the United States. She combined several dance forms—classical ballet, jazz, and modern—mixing them together with a vibrant and witty style. Twyla dislikes giving her unique style of dance any label, reasoning, "I simply think of it as dancing. I think of it as movement."

Twyla is known for being a serious, forthright, and diligent worker. In the face of many odds, she forged her own dance company in the late 1960s, for which she choreographed, managed, and danced. The noted troupe—famed for such jazz ballets as *The Bix Pieces*, *Eight Jelly Rolls*, and *Deuce Coupe*—lasted until 1988. Tharp later revived the troupe with fewer dancers.

Early on, Twyla realized that her performance group needed a large audience base to stay operational. Thus, she frequently choreographed her pieces to pop music (and sometimes to classical works), which brought her to the attention of a wide slice of the public and made critics take note of her innovative dance creations. She gained further renown by choreographing for such famous companies as the American Ballet Theatre, the Joffrey Ballet, and the Paris Opera Ballet. She also claimed the spotlight for her work in the mid-1970s (and thereafter) with Mikhail Baryshnikov, the remarkable Russian dancer who had defected to the West while touring with the Kirov Ballet.

Twyla is a strong advocate for increasing public recognition of dance as an art form. She has said, "I feel that dancers are certainly the equivalent of athletes [and movie stars]. . . . I want our culture to acknowledge them." She reasons, "Why shouldn't we be acknowledged for what we do, what we bring, and the value we have in a culture." However, except for very young artists just starting out, Twyla feels that dance should not be considered a charity case when it comes to raising funds. She says, "I feel that art has a responsibility in this culture to pull its own weight." As such, over many years, Twyla has reached out to other mediums—including film, television, and book writing—to generate money for her artistic ventures. Tharp's esteemed dance company was the first modern dance troupe to pay its dancers 52 weeks a year. With Twyla's example, other dancers and choreographers were inspired to pursue commercial exposure and success.

A Hard Worker with a Fast Mind

Twyla has long been known for her active and innovative way of thinking. As Marcia B. Siegel wrote in the *Boston Phoenix*, "Twyla Tharp doesn't realize that her mind is capable of processing three times more information than even the most above average audience member. It's part of her charm that she just assumes we can keep up with her."

Twyla's innovative way of thinking serves her well as she develops her ideas into completed choreographed works; this is usually a long, arduous creative and physical process for both her and her dancers. According to Tharp, "Preparation, hard work, and good habit . . . these things are absolutely necessary to anyone wanting to accomplish something, whether the creation of a dance or the proposal of a new product." It is Twyla's belief "that everyone is gifted, everyone is talented, and it is just a question as to how does one want to pursue this and how committed is one willing to be."

In her self-help book, *The Creative Habit: Learn It and Use It for Life* (2003), Twyla calls upon her decades of experience to determine that 10 factors (body, ambition, ideas, passions, needs, memories, goals, prejudices, distractions, and fears) are "at the heart of who I am. Whatever I'm going to create will be a reflection of how these have shaped my life, and how I've learned to channel my experiences into them." Tharp has also said, "I'm a great believer—though not a great lover—of failure."

A Leader in Her Field

Twyla has choreographed more than 125 dance pieces to date, and she has accumulated an array of trophies (including Tonys, Emmys, and *Dance Magazine* awards).

Among her many awards was one from Brandeis University in 1972. The university honored Twyla with its first Creative Arts award for dance, citing, "Her concern with movement as a superb expression of human creativity is reassuring to the audiences who admire this impressive documentation that the future of dance is in gifted and deeply committed hands." In 1992 Twyla was awarded a MacArthur Foundation "genius" grant and, seven years later, was named one of the Dance Heritage Coalition's first 100 "Irreplaceable Dance Treasures."

As Catherine Thomas of the *Oregonian* summed up, "For almost four decades Twyla Tharp has been a rebel with a single cause: Advance dance, no matter which choreographic taboos are broken, no matter the scarcity of funding, no matter what the critics say."

On one occasion the highly motivated Tharp said, "I had to become the greatest choreographer of my time. That was my mission and that's what I set out do." The Academy of Achievement agreed with her goal and, in 1993, inducted her into its honor roll of achievement. The organization reasoned

> No one making serious dances in this country since the 1960s could ignore the challenge of her inventive, quirky, complex creations. No serious dance artist

*Twyla Tharp accepts the Tony Award for Best Choreography
of a Musical for her Broadway show* Movin' Out.
(Associated Press)

has ever stretched the boundaries between classical and poplar, serious and silly, accessible and intellectual, as Twyla Tharp has. . . . When she first began to work with her own small company in the 1960s, Twyla Tharp brought more intelligence, humor, originality, and nerve to the making of dances than New York had seen in a long time, and she did it at a time when New York was the undisputed dance capital of the world. . . . Her place in dance history is secure.

2

A SPECIAL CHILD

Twyla Tharp was born on July 1, 1941, in Portland, Indiana. She was the first of five children of William and Lecile Tharp, who were Quakers. William operated a car dealership that leased farm equipment. He also ran a construction firm and other small-town enterprises. Lecile gave piano lessons to local youngsters.

From the start, Mrs. Tharp was convinced that her firstborn was extremely special and would "grow up to be famous . . . of that we've no doubt." Lecile named her child after Twila Thornburg, the Pig Princess of the 89th Annual Muncie (Indiana) Fair. Mrs. Tharp changed the spelling of Twila to Twyla to make it look more special when, assuredly one day, it would be a name the world would know.

An Early Love of Music

Soon after Twyla's birth Mrs. Tharp returned to her piano teaching. Thus Twyla, who was always near her mother, was exposed to music from nearly the start of her life. Tharp recalls in her autobiography, "Music seemed as much a part of my mother as her voice or her touch. To this day, whenever I hear Mozart or Bach—and Gershwin, Fats Waller, and Cole Porter too, for my mother practiced Tin Pan Alley as well as the classics—I feel loved."

As a very young child, Twyla spent many weeks each year staying with each set of her grandparents. These relatives worked hard on their Indiana farms, keeping their existences simple according to the beliefs of the Quaker religion, which does not permit the use of machinery. Twyla thrived in this unadorned atmosphere where "everything, including me, mattered." Here she learned that "elegance was efficiency."

When Twyla was one-and-a-half-years old Mrs. Tharp—who brought each of her children into the world of music at an early age—realized that her daughter had perfect pitch. As such, the musically gifted child was able to pick out the notes on the piano to match what her mother was singing. By the time Twyla was two, her ambitious mother was giving her piano lessons. Two years later, Twyla began taking piano lessons locally with Miss Remington, who specialized in instructing youngsters. This new teacher had a system in which she color-coded the piano keys to help her pupils to distinguish the notes and their contrasting audio impact. "To this day," says Tharp, "tones suggest both color and emotions to me." Meanwhile her mother had Twyla begin dance lessons, starting with tap and moving on to acrobatic and ballet dancing. Later came baton lessons as well as training in painting.

Twyla strove for the same perfection in her school lessons as she did in her musical and dance training. She soon discovered that attaining good grades was a way of connecting with her stern, hardworking father. She learned a parallel lesson about her mother. When Tharp was seven, she was entered in a piano competition given by the National Foundation of Music Clubs. At the contest, held in Indianapolis, Twyla emerged victorious in the junior division, winning out against rivals twice her age. Observing her mother's tremendous pride in this accomplishment, Twyla quickly appreciated that "it would be through performing that I could connect with her."

Caught in the overwhelming orbit of her determined mother, Twyla had then—and later—mixed feelings about her mother's ambitious educational plans for her. Tharp would later assess these plans. "She had a very specific idea about education, which was: You should know everything about everything. It was quite simple. There was no exclusivity, and there really was no judgment. . . . I think that I had a very eclectic and, in a way, a very democratic education. I'm grateful for that."

California, Here We Come

With the end of World War II in 1945 there was a new economic boom in the United States. A few years later the Tharps decided to move across country to California to provide their children with more cultural opportunities than Indiana had to offer. Because Twyla's mother was so enthralled with movies, the parents decided to build a drive-in movie theater in Rialto, a small desert town not too far from San Bernardino and about 46 miles east of Los Angeles.

The news of the impending move came as a great shock to young Twyla. Being the oldest offspring, she had the most friends and associations with her hometown, especially her beloved grandparents. But in August 1949 the Tharps packed up their possessions and drove to the West Coast. Imagining that she would now be living near the ocean, Twyla was dismayed to discover that their new home was to be in a tiny town far from the Pacific with a solitary main street and only three civic buildings: the police station, the bank, and the public library. The chief business in the area was growing oranges, and Twyla soon experienced—but never grew accustomed to—the sight and smell of the smudge pots used on cold nights to keep the fruit trees from damage.

The family eventually moved into their newly built home in an unpopulated area. The house happened to be constructed right over the San Andreas Fault (making it a perfect target for an earthquake) and nearby to the foothills (making the house a likely victim of the annual brushfires that ignited every fall in the local mountains).

Adjusting to her new life proved especially hard for Twyla. For one thing, her mother closely scrutinized the girl's grades. If they slipped below an A-, she marched into the teacher's office demanding to know why the instructor was incapable of teaching her child properly. As a result, over the coming years—between third and 12th grade—Tharp switched schools seven times. This created tremendous pressure on the eldest child to achieve perfection so that she would not be forced to transfer to yet another new school and begin the difficult adjustment process all over again. As an adult, Twyla would comment that being forced to be a scholastic overachiever made her dislike school. She says, "I hated the pressure of the situation, because I had to excel. It wasn't a choice on my part, it was expected."

Twyla's musical and dance education in California was even more intense than it was in Indiana. Her extracurricular studies now included a wide variety of dance lessons including ballet, toe, and flamenco, as well as violin, viola, and drum training, classes in painting, elocution, and shorthand, and special schooling in French and German. In her grand goal that her eldest child should be prepared for anything and everything, Mrs. Tharp drove her child here and there for instruction—often going on 100-mile commutes to benefit from the right teacher. With such a hectic curriculum, there was no opportunity for Twyla to socialize with her classmates outside of school. Mrs. Tharp encouraged this because she felt that socializing would only interfere with Twyla's other activities.

Having been bred on the extremely high expectations of her demanding mother, Tharp was not then aware how unusual her educational process was in its excessive quantity and variety. It became Twyla's "accepted" way of life, one in which she faithfully trusted that her parent "had some grand master plan we were accomplishing together."

Tharp later realized, "Childhood and the ability to socialize were taken away, eradicated from life. That's a stiff price to pay for the education that I received." On the other hand, she conceded, "I have the wherewithal to challenge myself for my entire life. That's a great gift."

Training with a Master

When Twyla was 12 she began studying ballet with Beatrice Collenette who, as a youngster, had been trained by the great Russian ballerina Anna Pavlova. Mrs. Tharp shepherded Twyla on the 200-mile round trip twice a week so that she could study with this classically trained dancer. With Tharp's natural aptitude and discipline, she soon was moved into the ballet school's upper class and was allowed to dance *on pointe* (the raising of the body on the tips of the toes). In her advanced sessions, each 90-minute lesson began at the barre (the horizontal wooden bar attached to the walls of the ballet classroom/rehearsal hall that the dancer holds for support) with warm-up and stretching exercises. Twyla, like the other advanced students, would respond to the instructor's orders spoken in French (the official language of ballet terms) to execute a *plié* (a bending of the knee or knees), a *demi-plié* (a half-bend), or *grande-plié* (a big bend). After such limbering up, the class would move away from the barre into controlled actions such as the *adagio* (slow and graceful movements done with agility), the *petite batterie* (lifting the body into the air with careful attention to foot articulation), and so forth.

When not having her many lessons, Twyla prepared at home for her next round of classes. At age 12, the youngster was undergoing a grueling schedule. A typical school day began at 6:00 A.M. and went nonstop until 9:30 P.M., by which time she had finally had her supper and went to bed. Her demanding timetable became her way of life, one in which, according to Twyla, "leisure, if it ever came, produced only dread. Recreation was completely foreign; it mystified me how kids could play together, simply inventing their days as they went along, not knowing each morning exactly how the day would unfold."

With such a packed program, Twyla remained isolated from her peers outside of the classroom. At home, she even found herself distanced from her younger siblings, who lived a far more carefree existence. Tharp soon took up residence in the guest wing of the sprawling family home and began to think of herself as an only child, one who dearly missed her kind grandparents and carefree friends back in Indiana. To fill her lonely "free" moments, Twyla occupied herself with reading. She read voraciously, including the Bible, which she read twice. For additional reading matter she turned to encyclopedias, classic novels, and even her mother's stash of popular adult fiction and magazines.

At school Twyla—who wore eyeglasses with pink metal frames and sported a pixie haircut—was branded a geeky bookworm. Shy and uneasy in the company of her classmates, the adolescent Tharp had no time or aptitude for dating or attending social functions.

The only outlet Tharp had from her unending studies was working at the family's drive-in theater, which she did every night during the summer and on weekends throughout the rest of the year. At the open-air movie theater she worked at the box office and snack bar. When she was not needed to sell tickets or food, she would watch the films unfolding on the big screen. In the process, Twyla developed a keen sense of what audiences liked and didn't like, a knowledge that would serve her well in her adult life.

A Natural Choreographer

As Twyla matured into a teenager, she began exploring dance steps on her own. These movements were not part of her many weekly lessons or preparations for recitals. She created these on her own, just to see what they would feel and look like. Sometimes to gain inspiration for her experimental work, she would rummage through a closet at home to find discarded garments that might become a makeshift costume and inspire her into new steps. Other times she would test her reaction to dancing on a different surface, such as a slippery floor, or how working in a big or small space might affect her physical movements. This investigation went on for countless hours throughout her teenage years.

One of Tharp's cherished childhood moments occurred one day when she was off by herself in a deserted part of the family property. As she sat reading a book, Twyla heard the distinctive sound of an approaching rattlesnake. Carefully picking up a hoe laying nearby, she bashed the snake in its head. She then draped the unconscious reptile over the branch of an olive tree. Tharp began dancing around the immobile snake, whooping it up as she circled it. Her excited cries soon brought her father into the yard. He noticed that the rattlesnake was reviving. He grabbed the hoe and knocked it to the ground, then cut off its head.

As Twyla later recalled of this exciting experience, "I had tapped directly into the primitive drive that celebrates brave physical conquest, good over evil, through ceremonial performances. I had created my first dance."

College Days

After graduation from Pacific High School in 1959, Twyla enrolled at Pomona College in nearby Pomona, California. Unsure if she had the talent to follow her growing desire to become a dancer, she registered as a premed student with thoughts of, perhaps, becoming a psychiatrist. Living on campus, she was now on her own, which was a totally new experience—both exciting and frightening. Almost immediately she felt unequipped to deal with the practicalities of independent life. While she was well trained in an assortment of artistic and academic areas, she knew little about life's everyday duties. It made her feel out of place in her new surroundings filled with such seemingly confident classmates.

Not long after moving into her campus dorm she met Peter Young. He was a Pomona College sophomore and a beatnik, artist, and renegade. He expressed an attraction for Twyla, and the duo soon became constant companions.

Following Twyla's freshman year at Pomona, Mrs. Tharp arranged for her daughter to spend the summer months in Los Angeles to pursue dance studies. Mrs. Tharp found and paid for her daughter's tiny apartment in Hollywood. In these weeks Twyla took ballet classes from a variety of instructors. Tharp continued to date Peter Young, who was spending the vacation months at his mother's home in nearby Santa Monica.

That fall, back on the Pomona campus, Twyla and Peter continued their romance. One day a school janitor came across the couple kissing in the school chapel. When the college's dean threatened Twyla with expulsion for the incident, Mrs. Tharp persuaded him to allow her daughter to transfer to Barnard College, a women's college affiliated with Columbia University in New York City. Pleased at the prospect of relocating to Manhattan, Tharp made no mention of the fact that Peter had enrolled at the Art Students League, also in New York.

Setting a New Regimen

With her grandmother Cora Tharp as her chaperone, Twyla set up residence in an apartment in Manhattan. Soon after starting at Barnard (her major was now art history), Twyla discovered that the campus dance classes (used to fulfill her physical education requirements) were not to her expectations. After meeting with her faculty advisers, she was granted the privilege of establishing her own dance curriculum with classes off campus.

Twyla studied with Igor Schwezoff (of the Kirov and the Ballets Russes de Monte Carlo) and Olga Pereyaslavec, both of whom also taught at the American Ballet Theatre. When Tharp found these classes too confining and impersonal, she sought other training grounds. She was disappointed to find that she could not gain admittance to the American School of Ballet, which prepared many candidates for working with the renowned ballet troupe of Russian-born choreographer George Balanchine. Initially disheartened not to experience Balanchine's guidance, Tharp acknowledged later, "Had I been allowed access to Balanchine, I probably would have signed up for life and never developed my own [style of dancing]."

Instead, Twyla enrolled in classes run by Richard Thomas and his wife, Barbara Fallis. Both were veterans of the American Ballet Theatre and the New York City Ballet. At her teachers' small studio, Tharp benefited from working out with such professional dancers as Cynthia Gregory and Toni Lander. Twyla soon realized that her unique background—filled with so many teachers and dance forms—seemed to put her at a slight disadvantage;

Twyla studied many different types of dance with different instructors. (Getty Images)

she did not have the focused mind-set of a classically trained dancer, who undergoes heavy-duty dance regimens and routines without question and unhesitatingly follows traditional movements. Tharp asked herself, "How could one become a classical dancer while at the same time asking what it means to move outside the regulation forms?"

To complement her dance classes, Twyla enthusiastically attended a wide sampling of dance concerts in New York City given by the companies of Merce Cunningham, Jerome Robbins, Alvin Ailey, Jose Greco, Anna Sokolow, and many others. As she experienced these exhilarating performances of varied dance forms, she constantly wondered if any of these forms should be a model for her own dancing. Wanting to test the creative options open to her, Tharp studied with several of these companies' lead choreographers. In particular, she studied with Merce Cunningham and Martha Graham, two of the pioneers of modern dance.

At the time Tharp began working with Graham in the summer of 1961, Graham was 67 and about to stop teaching on a regular basis. Nevertheless, Twyla learned a great deal from Graham's highly disciplined sessions. Eager to experience additional instruction, Twyla was creatively stimulated to work with Cunningham, a former Graham troupe member. Merce, according to Tharp, was less concerned with established traditions and more focused on "how we walk and run. He employed a technique poised between [traditional] ballet and Graham." Always exploring her dance options, Twyla also studied jazz with Eugene "Luigi" Lewis, which exposed her to steps frequently used in flashy Broadway stage productions.

With her diverse curriculum of dance forms and teachers, Twyla was intuitively participating in a new trend, especially among American dancers—that of the "crossover" dancer who was capable of performing any technique. Tharp was embracing a new dance language, one "capable of saying new things—or old things in new ways."

Looking to her future, the highly motivated, enthusiastic Tharp realized, "I was beginning to imagine a special niche for myself, a place in this swirling kaleidoscope of [dance] choice that no one else could fill, a kind of dance no one else could do."

3

THE BUDDING DANCER

During her years at Barnard College, Twyla's independent dance training continued at many classes around Manhattan. Besides Martha Graham and, later, Merce Cunningham, Twyla studied with modern dancers Carolyn Brown, Alwin Nikolais, and Erick Hawkins, and she had ongoing jazz sessions with Eugene Lewis.

As Tharp underwent her daily regimen of two or three dance classes, she formed theories about the traditional art form of movement. She would recall, "I couldn't bear the attitude. . . . I couldn't understand the fact that ballet was *about* going through certain conventions—the word *convention* in itself takes care of it. Ballet had become like the decorative art on Greek temples: just remnants of a past that nobody really understood anymore." Despite her doubts about traditional ballet, Twyla continued to take classical as well as modern and jazz sessions.

Marriage Intervenes

Between Tharp's hectic schedule of college studies and dance classes, she continued to see her boyfriend, Peter Young—despite her grandmother's efforts to keep the couple apart. Twyla and Peter married in 1962. Once the couple decided to start living together, Twyla's grandmother returned to Indiana.

Twyla graduated from Barnard in the spring of 1963, but chose to miss her graduation ceremonies because she was in rehearsal with Paul Taylor's dance troupe. Tharp would acknowledge later that she had not been picked by Taylor to join his company, but had just started appearing at his studio, where she would sit in a corner to observe his technique. When she saw him perform with Martha Graham's troupe on Broadway during her senior year at Barnard, his audacious stage performance helped Twyla decide that she wanted to dance professionally.

Having made herself known to Taylor, the persistent Twyla eventually was rewarded with the opportunity to be in one of Paul's dances, *Scudorama* (1963). Tharp's brief participation consisted of crawling across the stage beneath a large beach towel. Despite the brevity of her assignment, Tharp was thrilled to make her professional debut. Later in the year Twyla was allowed to perform in 16 of the Taylor Company's performances, using the stage name Twyla Young.

Once Twyla graduated from college, she and Peter rented loft space on Franklin Street in downtown Manhattan. The space boasted few living amenities but was large enough for Peter's painting studio and for Twyla to have a sizable dance practice area (20 × 17 feet). Their neighbor was painter Bob Huot, who would soon play an important role in Twyla's life.

Sorting Out Life

By the fall of 1963 Paul Taylor was creating a new dance piece (*Party Mix*). Twyla watched with great concentration as Paul developed the work. In her opinion, Taylor was veering further into theatrics and ignoring many established principles of dance. Her growing reaction to Paul's choreography style created a growing rift between the two artists.

Meanwhile, Peter Young was drafted into the Army and departed for training at Fort Dix in New Jersey. Feeling alone and adrift, Twyla began spending more time with artist Bob Huot. In the coming weeks, their relationship intensified and, eventually, she informed Peter Young that their marriage was over. The couple later divorced.

With Bob as her guide, Tharp now explored the art world, ranging from gallery exhibits and avant-garde films to bars frequented by painters, sculptors, and experimental artists.

In this period, the friction between Twyla and choreographer Paul Taylor grew, especially during a London tour. When the company returned to America that fall, Tharp left the group. Twyla and Bob Huot decided that New Year's Eve to live together.

As committed as she was to Huot, Twyla was more dedicated to her art. She wanted to dance professionally. Determined to earn her own way, Tharp began auditioning for ballet companies but soon realized that she lacked the years of focused classical training she needed in order to be accepted. Besides, it irked her to think she would be merely one of many doing the same steps in a ballet chorus. She went after job openings in TV commercials, industrial shows, and nightclub work, and she even applied to the famed Radio City Rockettes. However, she was defeated by her small frame and by her too-serious demeanor: She never smiled on stage.

Desperate for work, Twyla realized that if she wanted to perform, she must create her own work. This led to her first dance presentation on April 29, 1965, at Manhattan's Hunter College. The showcase was in a small auditorium in the school's art department where Bob Huot was an instructor. Her seven-minute piece was *Tank Dive*, featuring one dancer (Twyla) and four non-dancers (including Bob Huot). The piece utilized a recording of British pop singer Petula Clark's song

"Downtown." The title *Tank Dive* came from Tharp's belief that her venture in choreography had as much chance of success as one would have diving from a high platform into a teacup of water.

The morning after *Tank Dive* debuted to an audience of 12, naive Twyla rushed out to a local newsstand to buy newspapers and look for reviews of her debut. To her amazement, the publications contained no critiques of her presentation. At that moment, she was crushed. Much later, however, she realized it had been a blessing. She reasoned, "Today I'm grateful for the relative obscurity of my first five years as a choreographer. I had time to develop my own background, to find what I deemed important without having to cater to public taste." It gave her the freedom to experiment in new directions without fear of having to please others.

Moving On

Undaunted by the lack of critical response to *Tank Dive*, Twyla choreographed more dance pieces (including *Cede Blue Lake*) in 1965 and made a 16-minute dance film (*Stride*). To pay her bills, Tharp worked at the World's Fair in the Alaska exhibit and toiled as an office temp. She continued with her dance classes. As time passed, she realized that every aspect of her life was focused on dance; everything she did and everyone she interacted with was viewed in terms of what it taught her about dance and how she could use it in her next work.

With her total absorption in dance, her personal life with Bob Huot suffered. He suggested they marry, but having had a poor experience with her first marriage, she vetoed the idea. Returning to her main occupation—creating new dances—Twyla felt the need to include other dancers in her productions. She turned to Margaret Jenkins, a former Merce Cunningham studio member who agreed to work with Tharp for no pay. Margaret introduced Twyla to Sara Rudner, who auditioned for and joined Tharp's troupe. In the process of reluctantly accepting these two members into her dancing space, Twyla learned that "developing dance means developing dancers—the two are inseparable, and anyone who attempts to bypass this step is kidding himself. . . ."

With Margaret and Sara, Twyla rehearsed for the next seven months, working at least four hours a day, six days per week. They found free practice space at Manhattan's Judson Church gym, which brought the trio into proximity with more established, older dance forces who frequently dismissed the three women as upstarts.

The group's _Re-Moves_ (1966), presented in a performance space at the Judson Church, was divided into four parts, with the three women dressed largely in black (since the piece focused on death). The innovative dance piece filled with horizontal and vertical moves actually received reviews. Clive Barnes (*New York Times*) wrote, "Miss Tharp herself is so cool she could use a refrigerator for central heating." Of Twyla's choreography, Barnes assessed she was "bad in a rather interesting way." Other critics were intrigued by Tharp's innovative dance steps, which sampled many forms, including tap dancing. Few reviewers claimed to be impressed by the untraditional piece. But they were curious to see what Twyla Tharp would do next on the dance stage.

Stirred by her work at the Judson, Twyla ambitiously thought she and her troupe should embark on a European tour. Thanks to Bob Huot's contacts in the art worlds of Paris and London, Tharp arranged bookings at museums and galleries in those cities. With the help of two newly found patrons, Tharp's group also obtained some theater bookings abroad. To provide a second evening of repertoire (a list of performances) for the tour, Twyla created two additional pieces: *Jam* and *One, Two, Three*.

In February 1967 the dance trio flew to Stuttgart, Germany, for the start of its three-week tour. When the trek was over, Margaret remained in Europe. Back home Tharp added two new members to her organization: Theresa Dickinson and Margery Tupling. Having formed this quartet, Twyla was determined to keep it together. To do so meant

Twyla (center) is always looking to challenge her dancers and to keep her work fresh. Thus, she rarely reuses old dances when preparing a new program. (Photofest)

a pressured schedule of continually creating new dance pieces for the troupe to present publicly.

Twyla married Bob Huot in 1967. They were united in a civil ceremony at Manhattan's City Hall, with a small reception (including Mr. and Mrs. Tharp) at the Staten Island home of the groom's parents. Twyla insisted that she would retain her given name and that she would not wear a wedding ring. Having failed at a first marriage, she did not want to publicize her second.

Building a Career

With her life in a more settled mode, Twyla devoted the next year to developing new dance works for her troupe. She felt that each new work was another step toward better efforts, so she rarely reused old dances when preparing a new program. Exploring new and unusual dance theories and styles, she and the three other dance members spent hours trying new movements. They were building what Tharp called "harmonic possibilities." Nothing was too bizarre for the troupe to attempt. As they explored new steps, one of Twyla's rules was to avoid "unison movements," because she felt each member of her special group was too unique to be subjected to uniformity.

The quartet's debut was in April 1967 at the Bang Festival at the Richmond Professional Institute in Virginia.

They performed their piece *Disperse* in the college gym. By now, the troupe had learned the importance of not distancing themselves from their audience. They began to relish opportunities of dance innovation of any sort to keep viewers fully engaged in what was happening onstage. Tharp's husband, who often designed the sets for the dance performances, provided the costumes for *Disperse*. His wardrobe gave the performers a unique onstage look.

The quartet of dancers developed into a tight clique through long hours rehearsing together, driving to their next public engagements, and so forth. Their closeness paid off as they performed Twyla's intricate, demanding steps. Interacting on a close level with her dancers made Twyla realize how much of her life had been spent apart from her peers. She admitted that she had little real experience in communicating—especially making small talk—with others.

The troupe's next piece was *Generation* (1968). The *Village Voice* described the piece as "a lot of intricate run-jump-slide-hop-leap patterns and explosions . . . [leading] into wild flinging floppy gyrations with great complexities. . . . " In the coming months the dedicated troupe performed such new entries as *Excess, Idle, Surplus* (1968).

In this period Twyla added three additional members to her dance team. This required a time-consuming audition process and period of group adjustment. As before, all the women bonded, driven by their mutual desire to make innovative dance. In order to practice, the women moved around the city to wherever they could find free or inexpensive rental space.

In a review of the troupe's 1969 piece *After "Suite,"* Deborah Jowitt of the *Village Voice* described Twyla's unique style as follows: "Twyla Tharp has changed a lot since I last saw her work in 1966. She has purged her dances of almost every element but movement. . . . She has been able to do what I thought might be impossible; she has transferred her own incredible style to her company. . . . This style . . . involves acquiring a strong classical technique and then learning to fling it around without ever really losing control. The dancing is difficult, quirky, beautiful, stylish."

With each new project, Twyla and her ensemble were gaining increasing recognition. But this also brought the pressure of improving upon their past work. Always seeking to blend dance movements with the special requirements of the space where they were performing, Tharp staged *Medley* (July 1969) outdoors at New London's Connecticut College. The work was commissioned by the American Dance Festival, which allowed Twyla and her troupe to budget a $30 weekly salary for each dancer for 20 weeks. (Thereafter, the dancers were entitled to apply for unemployment payments.)

One of the unique aspects of _Medley_ was that, for the first time, Tharp did not perform in the production. She wanted to view the piece as part of the audience. The experience taught her that not being part of the dance was frustrating. She also discovered that being among viewers as they commented on the proceedings made her uneasy. By the time _Medley_ was restaged for Central Park in September 1969, two members of the troupe had left, and Twyla had decided to return to being an onstage performer.

Twyla felt abandoned (and betrayed) by the dancers who left the troupe. She explored her mixed emotions in her next work, _Dancing in the Streets_, done in Hartford, Connecticut, in November 1969. Before the presentation began at the Wadsworth Atheneum the cast warmed up in front of the museum, requiring the perplexed ticket holders to walk through the dancers to reach their theater seats. Later, _Dancing in the Streets_ was restaged at Manhattan's Metropolitan Museum and was reconfigured to take advantage of the new space.

Becoming increasingly adventurous in her creative efforts, Twyla's next offering was 1970's _Pymffyppmfynm Ypf_ (the bizarre title was the result of a typo in the _New York Times_). The piece was given at an all-women's school in Virginia. Tharp and her troupe were annoyed by the fact that the girls' institution had a male dean. In protest, one of the dancers performed her solo first topless, then bottomless.

Having worked doggedly and innovatively for five years—gaining a growing professional reputation in the process—Twyla was frustrated that she had such difficulty making her small group financially self-sufficient. Although the organization accepted commissions and Tharp constantly applied for grants, their monetary situation was constantly touch and go. All the dancers had sacrificed their personal lives and financial well-being to a great degree, which eventually caused them great stress. This made Twyla, their leader, feel guilty. Making matters worse, several of the members were forced to depart, either from dance injuries or, in the case of two individuals, from work visas expiring.

In the midst of Twyla's discouragement in early 1970, her husband was submitted for and received a grant from the National Endowment for the Arts. With the sudden funds on hand, the couple agreed to make a dramatic change in their lives. They purchased a large farm, with a farmhouse, barn, and huge acreage, in upstate New York. That May, now settled into their new lifestyle, Twyla discovered she was going to have a baby.

4

MAKING HER NAME

During the summer of 1970 Twyla was adjusting to her life on a farm, with all its daily demands. She believed that her dancing and choreographing days were now behind her. She devoted herself to helping her husband, Bob, renovate their farmhouse and spent many hours searching for antiques with which to decorate their new home. A few days each week, Bob drove into Manhattan to teach his art classes at Hunter College. This income helped to pay for the couple's necessities on the farm.

However, after experiencing just six weeks of such country living, Twyla felt her very busy life was somehow incomplete. It prompted her, with Bob's help, to convert the large attic of their house into a dance studio. Once the rehearsal space took shape, Twyla invited two women from her Manhattan dance troupe to join her on the farm. (A third female dancer, a newcomer, soon was added to the group and boarded in a nearby rented house.) For a time, it seemed an ideal existence for the women, who both worked on the farm to sustain themselves and spent hours practicing dance in their private studio.

Tharp was creatively productive. She discovered that her farm chores constantly inspired new dance moves. Twyla remembers, "Everything from sweeping out corners to thinking about the workings of a compost heap gave me new elements and purposes for the dances."

Although pregnant and loaded with farm duties, Twyla accepted the challenge of preparing a dance program in August 1970 for presentation at the University of Massachusetts at Amherst, where she agreed to be in residency that summer. Among the new works presented, which included *Rose's Cross Country* and *The One Hundreds*, the most important entry was *The Fugue*. Inspired by past choreography of the innovative George Balanchine, Twyla strove to make this key piece a "rigorous, accurate, authentic, elegant, original dance."

After the Amherst performance, Twyla and her troupe performed *The Fugue* and *The One Hundreds* at the outdoor Delacorte Theater in Manhattan's Central Park. *The Fugue*, in particular, received a healthy, positive response from the audience. But true to the group's austere tradition, the dancers took no curtain calls. However, Tharp was now inspired to interact more with the audience, to make them greater participants in the proceedings. This led her to staging (parts of) dances among passersby when the dance was given in an outdoor space. Or, in the case of *The One Hundreds*, recruiting audience members to be (minor) participants in the actual proceedings.

A New Breed of Teacher

While spending long stretches at the farm located near New Berlin, New York, Twyla noticed that her dancers were becoming restless. These lengthy isolation periods made them miss their personal lives in the city. In reaction to her dancers' discomfort, Tharp tried a system of dividing her expanding group into two teams: While one was rehearsing daily on the farm, the other would be in the city, and then the squads would switch locations. Soon, however, workaholic Tharp found herself wanting all the dancers on hand all the time so everyone could participate on the new works in progress and she could see the full impact of her latest choreographed moves.

One useful innovation for the daily dance workouts—especially helpful as Tharp grew increasingly incapacitated by her pregnancy—was the use of a secondhand videotape system. Thus, while she personally trained one group, the other would study a cassette of dance movements that Twyla had taped.

Twyla's choreographing in late 1970 led to *The History of Up and Down, I and II* and *Eight Jelly Rolls*. Both were presented at Oberon College in Ohio in January 1971, where Tharp was undertaking a brief on-campus residency.

Family Changes

Returning from Ohio back to the farm, Twyla gave her dancers a vacation while she waited out the final weeks of her pregnancy. Her son, Jesse Alexander Huot, was born in March 1971. Several days after the birth, Tharp's parents arrived from California for a visit. During the visit, Mr. Tharp was arguing with Bob Huot and started to experience severe chest pains. He was rushed to a local hospital. By now he had suffered a new stroke (several minor ones over past years having gone undetected) and was partially paralyzed. Later, he returned to Twyla and Bob's farmhouse. A few days thereafter, Mr. and Mrs. Tharp went to stay with their daughter Twanette at her home in Vermont. Subsequently Mrs. Tharp returned to the West Coast to handle family business while her husband, unable to travel, remained in Vermont. A few weeks later, William Tharp died of an aneurysm.

Twyla and baby Jesse flew to California to be with her mother during this difficult transition period. But even this recent family tragedy could not bridge the huge emotional gulf between Twyla and her parent. During this difficult visit, Tharp sensed another chapter in her life was closing and that now she had to be her own person—emotionally self-sufficient. This was confirmed when she returned to the farmhouse and grasped that her father's death had furthered the growing distance between her and her strong-minded husband.

Tharp found it difficult to balance her new role as mother with that of being a wife and a passionate, ambitious dancer. While regaining her physical and emotional strength after the pregnancy, she began to choreograph new pieces. In addition, she pushed forward with a mountain of paperwork to help establish a nonprofit foundation for her dance troupe.

In late May 1971 Twyla and her dedicated dancers performed their new piece, *Torelli*, at an outdoor site in Manhattan. Soon thereafter, Tharp discovered that she was again pregnant. While Bob wanted this new child, Twyla did not and had the pregnancy terminated. This act created further rifts in Twyla's troubled marriage. Adding to Tharp's marital woes were the many differences of opinion between her and her husband. This included his hatred of commercialism and any political control of his art. She, on the other hand, was far more practical and willing to do what was necessary to make her dance troupe financially self-sufficient.

Twyla is a demanding choreographer who has always believed in the purity of dance itself. In her early performances she rarely tried to engage the audience. (Getty Images)

The Sound of Music

During the first years of Twyla's choreographing, she had generally avoided the use of music in her rigorous, unadorned dance works. She was striving for purity of the dance form and did not want the intrusion of other arts. Now she changed her mind, feeling that music, albeit "old hat" in tandem with dance, would make her works more accessible to audiences. Her husband, Bob, took this as another sign of his wife selling out to commercialism.

During the summer of 1971 Tharp reworked *Eight Jelly Rolls* to add the taped accompaniment of music (a blend of ragtime and New Orleans jazz) once recorded by the late Jelly Roll Morton and his musicians. The revamped work was presented successfully that September as part of the New York Shakespeare Dance Festival. (*Eight Jelly Rolls* was later taped for British TV presentation in 1974.) By now Twyla was too busy with her work to continue making the long commute between the farm and New York City. She and little Jesse stayed full-time at a loft apartment in downtown Manhattan.

Thanks to the great reviews for *Eight Jelly Rolls*, Tharp and her company were increasingly in demand in the dance world. Inspired by this success, she broke another of her long traditions—that of using only women in her dance company. Appreciating the different dimensions that male dancers could add to her troupe, she persuaded Kenneth Rinker, a former Merce Cunningham dancer, to join her ensemble. With the addition of Ken and other male dancers, it made logical sense to choreograph dance partners into the new works. This fresh direction added new complexities and directions in Twyla's choreography.

Still missing her father, Twyla was inspired to create a dance piece that would utilize the music of Bix Beiderbecke, the famed American jazz musician and composer who Mr. Tharp must have heard as a young man. This developed into Twyla's *The Bix Pieces*, which premiered in November 1971 at the IX International Festival of Dance in Paris. For this tour abroad, Tharp left Jesse on the farm with his dad and her grandmother. Designer Kermit Love provided the stylish wardrobe for Twyla's new presentations, and the female dancers received chic hairstyles to further the troupe's new fashionable look. *The Bix Pieces* also utilized a narrator, an addition that would help the audience better comprehend the piece. *The Bix Pieces* was well received in France and, thereafter, in later presentations.

Returning to America in late 1971, Twyla and her husband realized that their marriage had passed the point of repair. They decided to end their union, with Jesse now residing with Twyla permanently in her Manhattan loft.

Financial Struggles

As 1972 progressed the now single Twyla, who received child support but no alimony from her ex-husband, focused on the difficult task of keeping herself and her dance group afloat. She increased the number of engagements at which her dancers performed. The group often made long commutes for such appearances. She pushed for new grants and commissions. Tharp also added a group of young dancers—called the Farm Club—to handle additional, lesser presentations. Meanwhile, in April 1972,

In the early 1970s, Twyla started choreographing pieces that included both men and women. (Getty Images)

Tharp received her first award, a citation from Brandeis University. It was to be the first of many awards she would receive over the years.

Distracted by supervising her many dancers and still sorting out a personal life that included her baby boy, Twyla's only dance premiere in 1972 was *The Raggedy Dances*. It utilized the contrasting music of ragtime king Scott Joplin and classical composer Wolfgang Amadeus Mozart. The piece bowed at Broadway's ANTA Theater that October and was well received.

Meanwhile the esteemed choreographer Robert Joffrey had seen a restaging of *The Bix Pieces* in Central Park and commissioned Tharp to create a new work for the Joffrey Ballet. Realizing the importance of this golden opportunity, Twyla went into overdrive. She wanted to provide the Joffrey with an innovative work that would make full use of the troupe's talent. Initially she thought of setting her work to the music of the Beatles, of whom she was a great fan. Then she had a change of creative mind, preferring to use the songs of the Beach Boys, the ultimate surf band in America.

Utilizing core members from her own group, Twyla was faced with the challenge of guiding the Joffrey troupe into her style, while leading herself and her dancers into the more traditional ways of the Joffrey. As Tharp progressed with training the two camps in her new work, she had a further inspiration. One night while riding a New York subway, she was struck by the creativity of young graffiti artists who had spray painted the train cars. She hired six such teenage graffiti talents to appear onstage during the performance and spray paint a 15-foot roll of paper, which became part of the piece.

The completed work, *Deuce Coupe,* premiered in Chicago in February 1972. Of the debut one reviewer wrote, "Twyla Tharp's *Deuce Coupe* is the best thing to have happened to the Joffrey Ballet in a long time. It is also one of the best things to have happened to dance in America." The work became a sell-out attraction wherever it was performed in the United States and abroad. Unfortunately, in the process of touring with the Joffrey, Twyla became disenchanted with the high-profile troupe's audience-pleasing efforts. She was also disheartened by the often-freewheeling lifestyle on the road of some Joffrey members, which conservative Tharp found unappealing. It led Twyla and her dancers to separate from the Joffrey at the end of their tour.

However, as Tharp and her core group forged ahead in mid-1973 as the Twyla Tharp Dance Foundation, she accepted a new commission from Robert Joffrey for his troupe. Needing the money and exposure it would provide, she was happy to learn that this time around she would be choreographing solely for the Joffrey group; she did not having to integrate her own dancers into the mix.

Utilizing Franz Joseph Haydn's 45th Symphony ("The Farewell Symphony"), Tharp created *As Time Goes By,* which she says was "anchored squarely in the traditional ballet vocabulary." She challenged herself artistically by confronting gender stereotypes. As such, the female dance lead was the strong force of the piece, as opposed to the softer male key role. The work premiered to positive response at New York City Center in October 1973.

More Transitions

The year 1974 was productive and hectic for Twyla. She and her group performed onstage in London and taped two television dance specials while there. She also put together a multimedia project (*All About Eggs*) commissioned by a Boston PBS-TV station.

During this busy period, Twyla's dance group dwindled down to three dancers and Twyla. Twyla accepted a commission (as part of a residency program) in Minneapolis/St. Paul, Minnesota. For the occasion she created *Sue's Leg,* a tribute to the flavorful music of jazz musician Fats Waller, which was performed in February 1975. (The work would later air on the TV series *Dance in America.*) Tharp staged this zesty piece in a converted old firehouse. This made the presentation less intimidating to members of the audience who were not attuned fully to the world of dance. In a subsequent residency in Minnesota, Twyla

Twyla (second from right) and dancers on the television show
Dance in America (Photofest)

broke down the barriers between audience and dancers
further by inviting anyone to attend daily rehearsals of a
new piece.

At this time Rhoda Grauer became the Twyla Tharp
Dance Foundation's new executive director. She helped
the group to set a new fiscal policy. Grauer promised that,
somehow, each member of the troupe (including Tharp)
would be paid $250 weekly—every week of the year. This
was the first dance company in the United States to have
such a policy. Through much struggle, this innovative,
ambitious plan would be in effect for the next 13 years,

requiring a great deal of ingenuity and productivity to meet the weekly payroll.

Twyla's innovative work next led her into an unexpected new venue. She was asked by the directors of the acclaimed American Ballet Theatre to create a showcase for their remarkable young Latvia-born ballet star, Mikhail Baryshnikov, who had defected to the West in 1974.

Twyla Tharp's career was on the fast track to major success.

5

TELEVISION, FILM, AND BROADWAY

Choreographing a dance piece for the highly talented Mikhail Baryshnikov was a courageous step for Twyla Tharp. As she reasoned, "Yes, he guaranteed great exposure for the choreographer working with him. But notoriety can harm as well as help: If the work failed, the choreographer, not Misha [as he was called by associates and friends] would be blamed because he was already an untouchable." Gutsy and adventurous, Twyla moved ahead with the commission. As she notes in her autobiography, at least part of her motivation was Baryshnikov's good looks and charisma.

Choreographing Ballet's New Prince

As Twyla rehearsed with Mikhail and the other dancers in the summer and fall of 1975, she was glad that Baryshnikov wanted to expand his remarkable dancing into new idioms. She soon discovered, however, that the star sometimes had a short attention span. She reasoned that this was brought on by cultural adjustments to his new life and by his non-stop performance schedule.

To provide the structure for this crucial artistic venture, Tharp eventually chose Franz Joseph Haydn's Symphony no. 82 in C Major ("The Bear"). Fearful that relying strictly on the four movements of Haydn's work would not inspire Baryshnikov, Tharp inserted some jazz music ("Bohemian Rag") by Joseph Lamb. This required Baryshnikov to move away from his classical training and to think of his dance movements in terms of a polished stage and film dance star such as Fred Astaire. In the piece, Baryshnikov played with the affections of several women. He debonairly wore a bowler hat in the production to emphasize the charming nature of his character.

Titled *Push Comes to Shove*, the much-anticipated production debuted at the Uris Theater on Broadway on January 9, 1976. The piece met with great audience fervor and, at the enthusiastic curtain calls, Mikhail escorted Twyla onto the stage. Still dealing with her innate shyness at interacting with audiences, Twyla was reserved and contained. (However, at least she did not throw back into the audience a bouquet of flowers tossed to her in tribute, which she had done at the premiere of 1973's *As Time Goes By*.)

Appraising Twyla's avant-garde ballet *Push Comes to Shove*, Robert Coe writes in his book *Dance in America*: "More than any other contemporary choreographer, Tharp knew what artistic freedom was worth, answering not only to the timelessness of ballet but also to the needs and perceptions of her own era."

Tharp would reteam with Mikhail Baryshnikov for *Once More, Frank*, inspired by the songs of Frank Sinatra. The piece debuted at the New York State Theater in July 1976. During this fertile creative period, Twyla and her group experimented with a variety of dance forms. For example, *Give and Take*, which premiered at the Brooklyn Academy of Music in March 1976, was a tribute to the style of George Balanchine. *After All*, done in late 1976, was staged on ice at Madison Square Garden in Manhattan, featuring Olympic gold medal figure skater John Curry. *Mud* (1977) featured the troupe dancing in pointe shoes as well as Adidas sneakers. *Cacklin' Hen*, which debuted the same night as *Mud*, was Tharp's rendition of a traditional American country hoedown.

Hollywood Beckons

For PBS-TV, Twyla conceived and directed the TV special *Making Television Dance*, which aired in October 1977. To prepare for the 60-minute program, Tharp taped 75 hours of her troupe's work over a year's time, including bits and pieces of rehearsals and offstage respites. Despite the mixed reviews that *Making Television Dance* received, Twyla was eager to expand her knowledge of television (and film) techniques. Thus when Milos Forman, a Czechoslovakian-born movie director, approached Tharp with a career offer, she could not resist the new challenge. He had seen and enjoyed *Push Comes to Shove* and suggested to Twyla that she choreograph his upcoming film assignment. It was to be a screen adaptation of the long-running Broadway musical *Hair*, which had been given a then-impressive $11 million budget by United Artists Pictures.

Anxious to expand her creative horizons, generate cash for her Dance Foundation, and provide work for her troupe, Twyla accepted. Beginning in 1977 she began meeting with Forman as he and writer Michael Weller reshaped the stage hit for the big screen. Not long into the process of auditioning key performers for the project, Twyla learned an unfortunate truth about moviemaking: "Of all the elements that made up the [screen] musicals— book, music, dance—dance came last. Real dance passages never seemed to find a place in the story, and dancing ability was never considered in casting." Most of the cast was selected primarily for their cinematic look and/or acting presence, not their dancing ability.

During the production, Tharp had to adapt herself to the demands of director Forman, who was a tireless perfectionist. Although she could understand this trait in another artist, she found it difficult to have to surrender her creative thoughts to his final decisions in all matters about *Hair*.

Hair was filmed in several locations, including New York City, California, and Washington, D.C. During filming, Tharp experienced firsthand all the frustrating elements of major movie shoots. After all, she was used to setting her own schedule and having everything onstage under her control. Twyla found that her work—and life—during *Hair* had become "unreal." But she did find comfort in the fact that she could use many of her core dancers for the picture's elaborate musical numbers.

Hair debuted in March 1979 with much fanfare. Unfortunately, it was not a big success like other screen musicals of the time, such as *Saturday Night Fever* (1977) or *Grease* (1978). For Tharp, the poor reviews the film received were the final disappointment in a two-year project that had been time-consuming and creatively frustrating. Nevertheless, she did not give up on movies as an outlet for her talents. She hoped that the next time she would be better prepared to cope with the unique demands, politics, and artistic challenges of film. Thus, when Forman later asked her to choreograph dances in

A scene from Hair (Photofest)

the films *Ragtime* (1981) and *Amadeus* (1984), she accepted the offers.

Back to Basics

With *Hair* having consumed so much of her time in 1978, Twyla was eager to return to dance. In 1979 her dance piece *1903*, featuring music by Randy Newman, debuted at the Opera House of the Brooklyn Academy of Music.

On the same program were *Chapters and Verses* and *Baker's Dozen*. *Baker's Dozen* was unquestionably the big crowd-pleaser.

Always looking to explore new artistic paths, Twyla wanted to add the spoken word to her next piece. She felt this would characterize her life changes as she approached her 40th birthday as a single mother. In her latest piece, she turned to playwright Thom Babe for creative feedback. He suggested she use a poem by A. A. Milne in the performance, and he worked with Twyla to give her new dance work greater narrative structure. Entitled *When We Were Very Young*, the project premiered on Broadway's Winter Garden Theater in late March 1980. In *Dance Magazine*, Twyla said the following about this work: "The new piece represents a culmination, and if this does not turn out to be a developed and full and mature person performing in this new piece I will be very disappointed, because I have spent a lifetime getting here."

However, it was a companion piece, *Brahms' Paganini*, that became the hit of the program at the Winter Garden Theater. Many dance critics said it was brilliant. In contrast, *When We Were Very Young*, in which Tharp symbolically walked over the stage footlights and tumbled into the orchestra pit, met with harsh criticism from many reviewers. However, the piece sufficiently captured the public's fancy—especially that of women—and made a final profit of $5,000. Refusing to be set back by the mixed response to *When We Were Very Young*, Tharp remained active in self-producing her group's performances on the road.

In 1980 Tharp choreographed a piece (*Three Fanfares*) to be performed at the closing ceremonies of the Winter Olympics at Lake Placid, New York. She also provided *Dance Is a Man's Sports Too*, which aired on ABC-TV. The work accommodated performances by New York City Ballet dancer Peter Martins and Pittsburgh Steeler wide receiver Lynn Swann.

Assorted Quartets, which used traditional fiddle reels, was performed at the Saratoga Performing Arts Center in Saratoga Springs, New York, in late July 1980. Two months later Tharp and her group were onstage at the Opera House in Ghent, Belgium, with *Short Stories*, which used the music of the rock group Supertramp and of Bruce Springsteen. A few days later, on October 6, Tharp and company debuted *Third Suite* at the Théâtre Champs-Elysées in Paris. The piece used orchestral music of Johann Sebastian Bach.

The Catherine Wheel

Through her then close friend and business associate Bill Graham, Twyla came into contact with musician David Byrne. Twyla had asked Graham to suggest an up-and-coming music group to provide hip, commercial music for her next major dance piece. Bill mentioned the Talking Heads, a new wave rock group that had released its debut album in 1977. Their leader and solo artist was the innovative and well-regarded Byrne.

Soon after meeting Byrne, Twyla and he began their collaboration on what would become *The Catherine Wheel*. Byrne watched many videotapes of Twyla's work, and she listened to the Talking Heads' music. She was impressed with his use of a variety of instruments, such as the ukulele, the synthesizer, and basic percussion "instruments" such as pots and pans.

Over several months of 1981 in New York City and London, Tharp and Byrne—who each had very different artistic ideas—worked on the narrative, musical, and dance structure of *The Catherine Wheel*. The much-hyped production opened at the Winter Garden Theater on September 22, 1981. At 78-minutes with no intermission, it was Tharp's longest and most ambitious work to date.

The piece's title has many references, including that of Saint Catherine of Alexandria, who was martyred on a spiked wheel in 307 A.D. A Catherine wheel is also a type of firework, similar to a pinwheel. Catherine wheels were also traditional cartwheels once performed on Saint Catherine's Day, the Catholic feast day for unmarried women. The term Catherine wheel also had been applied to countries where the current government was always tumbling over into the next one.

All these references and images were incorporated into the heartfelt narrative of *The Catherine Wheel*. The piece focuses on a married couple and their not-so-bright off-

Twyla created The Catherine Wheel *with musician David Byrne (right).* (Photofest)

spring. Other onstage participants included a hysterical maid, a cute dog, a visionary poet, and a mysterious woman in red. These key roles were performed on an imaginative set by Tharp's group of core dancers.

Two years later *The Catherine Wheel* was restaged for British TV and also aired in the United States. Everyone was far more satisfied with the new rendition of this elaborate, symbolic dance piece. For the TV performance, Tharp was nominated for an Emmy Award in the category of Outstanding Achievement in Choreography. Although she lost the trophy, she had proven repeatedly that she was a strong presence in the dance world.

6

RISING TO THE TOP

After *The Catherine Wheel*, Twyla kept herself busy professionally. With her 11-year-old son, Jesse, in boarding school, she returned to what she did best—work. She agreed to costar onstage with Andre Gregory in *Bone Songs* (1982), a two-character play written by Gregory. The production ran for two months. Next, Tharp's *Nine Sinatra Songs* premiered in Vancouver, British Columbia, in October 1982, followed, a few days later, by a piece titled *Bad Smells*. Bouncing around the globe, Tharp later was in Prague, Czechoslovakia, working on the dance sequences with filmmaker Milos Forman for *Amadeus* (1984). (*Amadeus* proved to be a commercial success and would go on to claim six Academy Awards.)

In November 1983 Twyla was at the University of Texas in Austin for the premieres of her *Fait Accompli* and *Telemann*. *The Little Ballet* was performed in Minneapolis in

Gregory Hines and Mikhail Baryshnikov in the film White Nights, *which Twyla choreographed* (Photofest)

April 1984, with *Sorrow Floats* debuting at the American Dance Festival in Durham, North Carolina, that July. Also in this hectic time, she was in Europe to coordinate the dance sequences for *White Nights* (1985), a film starring Mikhail Baryshnikov and Gregory Hines.

In this enormously busy period Twyla was so often jumping from airport to airport and country to country that she estimated she had circled the globe more than five times. As she says, "My internal clock was so screwed up I had begun to feel that nowhere in the world was it night."

Winning Emmys and Singin' in the Rain

Continuing her successful working relationship with Mikhail Baryshnikov, Twyla mounted *Baryshnikov by Tharp with American Ballet Theatre*, which aired on PBS-TV in 1984. The special was part of the *Dance in America* series. It featured new stagings of *Push Comes to Shove*, *Sinatra Suite*, and *The Little Ballet*. This well-received program led to Tharp being nominated for an Emmy Award for choreography and winning two Emmys, for writing and directing.

At this time Twyla was also involved in another big career move: choreographing and directing the Broadway musical *Singin' in the Rain*. The stage musical was based on the 1952 feature film of the same name. The musical had already been performed successfully in London, and its creators hoped it would also be well-received in the United States.

Twyla welcomed the challenge of this mammoth project while managing her dance troupe. She was also attracted by her sizable fees, which would help pay off the deficit from 1981's *The Catherine Wheel*. Moreover, her income from this mainstream project would help provide her Dance Foundation with cash flow to pay its members' salaries.

Mikhail Baryshnikov and Elaine Kudo in Sinatra Suite
(Photofest)

In tackling the stage musical, Tharp had to follow certain artistic guidelines. The scripters, who had written the 1952 film, did not want to tamper much with one of their greatest successes. They had no plans to revamp any part of their script to *Singin' in the Rain*. Also, Tharp felt it would be foolish to delete any of the classic dance numbers that so many remembered with great fondness. Moreover, the Broadway show's producers would retain all rights to any original choreography used in the new production. Twyla had always retained full ownership of her dance creations, thus she did not feel inclined to create new dance movements for the numbers.

Twyla found it difficult to cast charismatic lead performers who could handle the show's song-and-dance demands and also attract theatergoers. Many of the high-profile Broadway talents turned down the key role of Don Lockwood. They feared being compared to the performance given 33 years earlier by Gene Kelly, which no one felt they could improve upon. In addition, it was difficult to translate the film's memorable rain-soaked main sequence—where the hero dances and sings his way through the title song—onto the Broadway stage. Film editing techniques had played a major part in the screen number, and there was no way to compensate for this in live theater.

Later, Tharp would recall another of her problems in staging *Singin' in the Rain*: "I had figured the acting would take care of itself and [I] put dramatic scenes at the bottom of my rehearsal list." To help the performances of the cast, many of whom were not noted for their acting abilities, Twyla had to sign on an acting coach. Relinquishing part of her authority over the show was painful for Twyla.

The word began to spread that *Singin' in the Rain* was in serious trouble. Reactions of preview audiences were generally not favorable. By now, too much had been invested

Donn Simione, Cynthia Ferrer, and Brad Moranz from the Broadway show Singin' in the Rain; *the production would be one of the low points of Twyla's career.* (Photofest)

in the project to stop it and it pushed forward—with last-minute revamping—to its July 2, 1985, opening at the huge Gershwin Theater. Critical response to the lavish musical was largely negative, with some calling it "Singin' Down the Drain" and "Twyla Tharp Under Water."

Despite the unenthusiastic reviews, *Singin' in the Rain* lasted for 367 performances. Deeply discouraged and embarrassed by her high-profile misstep, Tharp flew to Los Angeles, where she took an actor's workshop to learn more about acting and directing. As part of the process to renew her artistic energies, she changed her diet (which included eliminating alcohol and caffeine) and began yoga classes. She now felt ready to return to work. She vowed to herself, "Never again would I work in theatre without a certain shrewdness which survival—through success or failure—brings."

Pushing Ahead

While in Los Angeles, Tharp videotaped many of her own new dance improvisations and refined movements. With this fresh material, she returned to New York and began preparing a new dance work. She consulted on the piece with a longtime friend, composer Philip Glass. She convinced the busy musician to work with her on a score for what would become *In the Upper Room.* Inspired by china bulldogs and porcelain dragons, this story showcased contrasting sets of dancers in movements that demanded "endurance, power, speed, and timing."

With the preliminary work accomplished, Twyla began auditions. (In the wake of *Singin' in the Rain*, several of Tharp's troupe had retired.) As always, Twyla had certain prerequisites in choosing dancers: They must have strong technique, the willingness to work, a sharp imagination, and the flexibility and desire to try new dance approaches. Regarding her auditioning process, Tharp says, "The moment a dancer enters the studio and drops his or her dance bag and street clothes, I know if I can fall in love [with his or her energy and charisma]. It is just that unfair."

The nearly 40-minute long *In the Upper Room* was performed in August 1986 at the Ravinia Festival in Highland Park, Illinois. It met with an enthusiastic response. It became a crowd-pleaser in the replenished company's 1987 dance tour. Also on the program was *Ballare*, a more traditional ballet set to the music of Mozart.

The End of the Foundation

During the demanding 1987–88 tour, Tharp took stock of her situation. The ever-spiraling costs of maintaining her Dance Foundation was making her daily life complex and pressured. In order to support her organization, she had to have her group work constantly to become well-known performers that would attract audiences. To her dismay she discovered, "I could no longer afford the luxury of a marvelous green talent: If I'd been a kid in an audition, I couldn't have been hired by me."

In addition, Twyla recognized that the dance world had changed greatly since the mid-1960s. No longer did she have the luxury of nurturing newcomers—letting them gradually absorb the scope of her creative goals and come to know her extensive repertoire. Moreover, she thought that many dancers in the late 1980s were motivated by financial rewards and fame rather than by dance itself.

Federal and state grants for the arts had diminished continually throughout the 1980s, and obtaining grants was far more competitive and complex than in past decades. Tharp was increasingly unhappy at spending so much of her time as a fund-raiser rather than as a choreographer. In addition, the nonstop administrative duties required of her were crushing.

Weighing all the pros and cons, Twyla decided to disband her Dance Foundation, ending a remarkable 23-year run. Having made the decision, Tharp alerted her dancers in the fall of 1987 that, by mid-1988, the company would be no more. Twyla then began work on what would be the troupe's last new piece, *Bum's Rush*. It would debut in February 1989 under the auspices of another company.

The American Ballet Theatre

At this crucial time in Twyla's career, Mikhail Baryshnikov invited her to join the American Ballet Theatre (ABT) as an artistic associate. In July 1988 she took the post. During 1989 Twyla choreographed *Bum's Rush* (utilizing dancers from her old company), *Everlast* (based on a story about a boxer and a socialite), and *Quartet* (a large dance showcase, which debuted at the Theater for the Performing Arts in Miami Beach, Florida). In the midst of these presentations, Twyla accepted an invitation from the Paris Opera, where famed Russian-born dancer Rudolf Nureyev was the company's director. In the French capital she staged a very formal ballet, *Rules of the Game*. As always, Tharp thrived on multitasking the demands of her new and different dance pieces.

In 1989, three days after an all-Tharp evening was presented at the Metropolitan Opera, Baryshnikov left the ABT. Twyla's contract with the ABT was not renewed. She remained with the troupe for the six final months of her pact in order to conduct a summer workshop and prepare her final piece for the group. It was ironically titled *Brief Fling* and was performed in San Francisco in February 1990.

This latest career change forced Tharp to reevaluate her life. She was now approaching 50 and no longer per-

In the Upper Room, *performed at the Brooklyn Academy of Music* (Photofest)

forming that much as a dancer in front of audiences. Her son was nearly 20, and Twyla was still working out her relationship with her mother. Many of Tharp's dance idols (including Martha Graham and George Balanchine) had died, others were retired, and newcomers were already making a name in the field.

Twyla had grown tired of hiring herself out to established dance companies. She says she felt "restrained by the conditions that are required when you work with professional companies. They have repertory that must be maintained. They have rules. Audiences have expectations. I began to want to make material addressing none of this."

Unsure of her career options and determined to be more cautious about her personal relationships and career in the future, Tharp started the 1990s with great uncertainty.

7

STAYING SUCCESSFUL

In October 1991 Twyla Tharp was busily reshaping her career. She was determined to be in full charge of her future. After staging *Grand Pas: Rhythm of the Saints* at the Paris Opera, that same month she premiered *The Men's Piece* (in which she danced) and *Octet* at Ohio State University in Columbus, Ohio. The following January *Sextet* premiered at the New York City Center.

By now Twyla had pulled together a fresh group of dancers, calling upon three talents from her past company and assembling the others from the New York City Ballet, the Paris Opera Ballet, and from more than 3,000 audition candidates. Not wanting to be caught in the trap of a large organization again, she avoided the use of the word "company" in referring to her new, smaller group.

The Successful Author

Having the knack for showcasing her talents—and earning income—in a variety of media, Tharp next turned to the world of publishing. She signed a contract with Bantam Books to write her autobiography, *Push Comes to Shove*, which appeared in November 1992. The often candid and revealing book opens with Twyla's statement, "People ask, 'How do you make a dance?' My answer is simple. Put yourself in motion." The book was praised for its funny and earnest insights into Tharp's life and career.

From book publishing Twyla switched to the world of Hollywood movies. Moviemaker James L. Brooks asked Twyla to choreograph the dances for his upcoming movie *I'll Do Anything*. The film was a bittersweet story of romance and Hollywood.

When *I'll Do Anything* was test screened, audiences did not respond to the song-and-dance interludes. Columbia Pictures demanded that the musical numbers be deleted and that Brooks shoot new scenes to fill the gaps. In the final version, which did not contain Twyla's dance scenes, Twyla was not listed in the credits.

On a more positive note, during this period Tharp premiered several new ballets, including 1993's *Pergolesi*, *Bare Bones*, and *Demeter & Persephone*. She was represented on TV by the PBS-TV multipart documentary, *Dancing*

(1993), appearing in the segment, "The Individual and Tradition."

In the early 1990s Tharp received a series of tributes. In 1992 she received the New York City Mayor's Award for Arts and Culture and, the same year, was given the prestigious MacArthur Fellowship. In 1993 she was inducted in the American Academy of Achievement and was named Woman of Achievement by her alma mater, Barnard College. She also accumulated honorary degrees from various universities across the country.

The Master Choreographer

Twyla continued sending her dance troupe on road tours in the mid-1990s, often premiering new works, such as 1995's *American We* and *Jump Start,* and 1996's *The Elements*. Sometimes she found opportunities to accept lecture engagements and to conduct workshops. For such occasions, she would talk to the audience about her past and present works and the current state of ballet. Sometimes these talks and dance examples became miniature tours that previewed her new choreography.

As had been true for many years, Twyla's new works often blended the traditional with pop culture. Such was the case with 1994's *Waterbaby Bagatelles*, which was influenced by memories of Esther Williams, a movie star known for playing in musical films with extravagant aquatic numbers.

Twyla often found inspiration for her new dance creations in her own past experiences. For example, the gentle *Sweet Fields* (1996) recalled early American sacred music, especially the 18th-century hymns of William Billings, while *66* (1996) paid tribute to Route 66, the American cross-country highway that Tharp and her family (and countless other Americans) traveled in the 1940s and 1950s. For *Heroes* (1996), she again collaborated with Philip Glass. In explaining her attraction to working with Glass, Tharp said, "I find his music very kinetic, very understanding of the frequencies in music. It makes me want to move."

When the above trio of works was performed on tour at the Kennedy Center in Washington, D.C., in late October 1996, Jean Battey Lewis (*Washington Times*) remarked: "Even if she didn't break new grounds with these ballets, the evening's effect was to show us Miss Tharp wrestling with more overtly serious themes than in her earlier work."

In the early fall of 1997 Tharp's ensemble (now consisting of a dozen dancers) performed at New York's City Center. It was part of an international tour that had started on the West Coast in 1996. The repertoire included the world premiere of *Roy's Joys*, a jazzy tribute to the jitterbug dance of the 1940s and 1950s.

When the tour reached Boston in March 1998, Twyla added *Yemaya* to the bill. It utilized Cuban popular music and the spiritual music of Santeria (an Afro-Caribbean religion). *Yemaya* demonstrated that the middle-aged choreographer was keeping her creativity open to new influences and trends as well as drawing on rich experiences from the past.

In late April 1999, when Tharp was the guest of honor at the Museum of Contemporary Art in Los Angeles, one of the speakers, actor and dancer Gregory Hines, said of her, "She is modern dance." In accepting her trophy Twyla commented, "This award is an affirmation of me . . . and also dance. It makes it clear that this is work that nurtures the spirit like art and music do . . . so thank you."

Into the New Millennium

Proving that she was very much a part of the contemporary dance scene, Twyla provided the only new work of the 2000 winter season of the New York City Ballet. Her creation was *The Beethoven Seventh*. Later in 2000 came the lyrical *Mozart Clarinet Quintet K.581* and yet another debut, the passionate *Surfer at the River Styx*. This was followed in 2001 by *Known by Heart Duet*, *Westerly Round*, and *Hammerklavier II*. These contrasting pieces led Mindy Aloff of the *New Republic* to remark: "No choreographer at the ballet in the past quarter of a century has worked to become a classicist more diligently, . . . in more painstaking detail, and with more energy and optimism than Twyla Tharp." Aloff also said, "Tharp certainly trips herself up sometimes . . . but she approaches ballet very seriously, and her flaws are more interesting than most of her colleagues' achievements."

Movin' Out

Tharp had long smarted at the unhappy experiences she had endured with her 1985 Broadway musical, *Singin' in the Rain*. Now she chose to return to Broadway with a fresh concept. Sometime in 2000 it occurred to her that the songs of Billy Joel contained enough of a story to create a thematic stage show. She envisioned his songs being sung by an onstage pianist and vocalist accompanied by a band, while the characters danced through a story that covers the years 1967 to 1987. The narrative would focus on three young men and the women they fall in love with. When the male trio leaves to fight in the Vietnam War, the relationships change. How the various individuals survive—for better or worse—would provide the climax to the story line.

Having gained Billy Joel's approval to proceed with her idea, Tharp determined that in this production the characters would have no dialogue. She reasoned, "What were we doing before language evolved? We were communicating by movement, so when you can link into a subject where you get substance, you're speaking to people in a much more deeply emotional way."

Her cast of dancers was drawn from such companies as the American Ballet Theatre, the Joffrey, and Hubbard Street Dance Chicago. A critical point for the production was finding and hiring Michael Cavanaugh, a personable young singer and pianist whose vocal style greatly resembled Billy Joel. A nine-piece orchestra was put together to back Cavanaugh, who would perform from a balcony above the stage. On this show, Twyla's son Jesse served as a production assistant.

After a 10-week tryout in Chicago, *Movin' Out*, with its more than two-dozen Joel numbers, opened at Broadway's Richard Rodgers Theater on October 24, 2002. Ben Brantley of the *New York Times* said the musical was "Twyla Tharp's shimmering portrait of an American generation."

Movin' Out was not only a huge critical success but enjoyed great box-office business. At the 2003 Tony Awards, the show earned Tharp a nomination for Best Director and she received a Tony Award as Best Choreographer. She and *Movin' Out* won several other theater awards during the 2002–03 season. The production enjoyed a lengthy, profitable Broadway run and prompted both an American national touring company and planned editions abroad.

Billy Joel and Twyla take a bow after Movin' Out's *Broadway debut.* (Associated Press)

While Tharp was the hit of Broadway, she continued to mount dance tours with her troupes and to occasionally premiere new pieces such as *Even the King* (2003). Always full of creative energy, she turned her lifetime of dancing, choreographing, and teaching experiences into the basis for the book *The Creative Habit: Learn It and Use It for Life*, published in 2003. The book was noted for its insightful take on the creative process and Twyla's own struggles for success as an artist. Twyla dedicated this popular book to her parents and her son.

In a *U.S. News & World Report* interview about the book, Tharp says, "Art is work. It is not inspiration," and "Creativity is about questioning." In response to being asked, "Why does being creative matter?" Twyla responded, "So that you walk out the door believing in yourself a little bit more. So you believe that in any given day you've made more of it than it might otherwise have been. So that you do not take things for granted. Creativity, ultimately, is a way of saying thank you."

Dancing into the Future

Twyla has always been aware that dance is unique among the creative arts because it is so difficult to document. Thus, in recent years she has turned her attention to preserving and organizing visual records of her dance work. More than merely archiving examples of her creativity, she wants to create a library of her work to provide examples and training tools for future generations of dancers.

Looking back on her prolific, cutting-edge career to date, Tharp points out that in her choreography she has always—consciously or not—sought to reach the largest audience possible. She explains, "Growing up in a drive-in theater . . . which I did, means that you attach yourself to entertainment that's destined for the masses. And if you are very serious about something, as I have been about dancing, you believe that it should be available to very

large numbers of people—it's no different from what lots
. . . of artists have done."

Once when asked why she takes her life's work so seriously, hardworking Twyla Tharp answered, "It's not a question of enjoying or not enjoying. It's what I do." However, she remains very upbeat about her chosen profession. "My feeling about what dance is is optimistic, positive and forward-moving. I've been angry but it doesn't last, because I've been gifted with the ability to go into a studio and work. The force of what moving gives to the body comes to me and I feel better and I'm grateful and I know that's what I want to share."

TIME LINE

1941	Born in Portland, Indiana, on July 1
1949	Family relocates to Rialto, California, where Twyla's parents operate a drive-in movie theater
1959	Graduates from Pacific High School; enrolls at Pomona College in Pomona, California
1961	Leaves Pomona College; matriculates at Barnard College in New York City
1962	Marries artist Peter Young
1963	Graduates from Barnard College; joins Paul Taylor's modern dance troupe, but leaves the ensemble by year's end
1964	Marriage to Peter Young ends; begins working odd jobs in New York City while auditioning for dance assignments

1965   Begins choreographing dance pieces to showcase
her skills; dance premieres: *Tank Dive*, *Stage Show*,
Cede Blue Lake, and *Unprocessed*; film: *Stride*

1966   Dance premieres: *Re-Moves* and *Yancey Dance*

1967   With her small troupe of women dancers, embarks
on a three-week European tour; weds longtime
companion Bob Huot, an artist; dance premieres:
One, Two, Three; *Jam*; *Disperse*; *Three Page Sonata
for Four*; and *Forevermore*

1968   Dance premieres: *Generation*, *One Way*, and *Excess,
Idle, Surplus*

1969   Dance premieres: *After "Suite,"* *Group Activities*,
Medley, and *Dancing in the Streets*

1970   She and her husband move to a farm in New Berlin,
New York; dance premieres: *Pymffyppmfynm Ypf*,
Sowing of Seeds, *The Fugue*, *Rose's Cross Country*,
and *The One Hundreds*

1971   Birth of son, Jesse; father, William Albert Tharp,
dies; moves with son from farm to a loft apartment
in New York City; she and Bob Huot end their
union; begins paperwork to form the Twyla Tharp
Dance Foundation; dance premieres: *The History of
Up and Down: I and II*, *Eight Jelly Rolls*, *Torelli*,

Mozart Sonata K.545, and *The Bix Pieces*; videotape: *The Willie Smith Series*

1972   Receives the first of many awards, an accolade from Brandeis University; dance premiere: *The Raggedy Dances*

1973   Choreographs a work for the Joffrey Ballet; dance premieres: *Deuce Coupe* and *As Time Goes By*; television: *The Bix Pieces*

1974   Dance premieres: *In the Beginnings, Twyla Tharp and Eight Jelly Rolls*, and *Bach Duet*; television: *All About Eggs* and *Eight Jelly Rolls*

1975   Works with international ballet star Mikhail Baryshnikov; dance premieres: *Deuce Coupe II, Sue's Leg, The Double Cross, Ocean's Motion*, and *The Rags Suite Duet* [from *The Raggedy Dances*]

1976   Commissioned to choreograph a work for premier dancer Mikhail Baryshnikov at the American Ballet Theatre; dance premieres: *Push Comes to Shove; Give and Take; Once More, Frank; Country Dances; Happily Eve After;* and *After All*; television: *Sue's Leg: Remembering the Thirties*

1977   Receives an offer from filmmaker Milos Forman to choreograph his upcoming movie musical, *Hair*;

dance premieres: *Mud, Simon Medley,* and *Cacklin' Hen;* television: *Making Television Dance*

1979   Dance premieres: *1903, Chapters and Verses,* and *Baker's Dozen;* film: *Hair*

1980   Dance premieres: *Three Fanfares, Brahms' Paganini, When We Were Very Young, Assorted Quartets, Short Stories,* and *Third Suite;* television: *Dance Is a Man's Sport Too*

1981   Collaborates with musician David Byrne (the Talking Heads) on a new dance piece for Broadway presentation; receives *Dance Magazine* Award; dance premiere: *Uncle Edgar Dyed His Hair Red;* Broadway: *The Catherine Wheel;* film: *Ragtime*

1982   Dance premieres: *Nine Sinatra Songs* and *Bad Smells;* television: *Scrapbook Tape*

1983   Begins preparation for the Broadway production of *Singin' in the Rain;* dance premieres: *Fait Accompli, The Golden Section,* and *Telemann;* television: *The Catherine Wheel*

1984   Teams with choreographer Jerome Robbins to stage a new piece for the New York City Ballet; nominated for an Emmy Award for Outstanding Choreography for *The Catherine Wheel;* dance premieres:

The Little Ballet, Brahms/Handel, Sorrow Floats, Bach Partita, and *Sinatra Suite*; film: *Amadeus*; television: *Baryshnikov by Tharp* with American Ballet Theatre

1985 Broadway: *Singin' in the Rain*; film: *White Nights*

1986 Dance premiere: *Ballare*; television: *In the Upper Room*

1988 Disbands dance troupe after a 23-year run; accepts a position as artistic associate at the American Ballet Theatre

1989 Leaves her post at the American Ballet Theatre; dance premieres: *Quartet, Bum's Rush, Rules of the Game*, and *Everlast*

1990 Dance premiere: *Brief Fling*

1991 Newly formed, compact dance troupe begins touring; dance premieres: *Grand Pas: Rhythm of the Saints, The Men's Piece*, and *Octet*

1992 Autobiography, *Push Comes to Shove*, is published; dance premieres: *Sextet* and *Cutting Up*

1993 Inducted into the American Academy of Arts and Sciences and the Academy of Achievement; dance premieres: *Pergolesi, Bare Bones,* and *Demeter & Persephone;* television: *Dancing*

1994   Dance premieres: *Waterbaby Bagatelles; New Works; Twyla Tharp in Washington: Red, White & Blue;* and *Noir;* film: *I'll Do Anything*

1995   Dance premieres: *How Near Heaven, American We, Jump Start,* and *Mr. Worldly Wise*

1996   Dance premieres: *I Remember Clifford, The Elements, Sweet Fields, 66,* and *Heroes*

1997   Becomes an honorary member of the American Academy of Arts and Letters; dance premieres: *The Storyteller* and *Roy's Joys*

1998   Dance premieres: *Moondog, Sam and Mary, Yemaya, Known by Heart,* and *Diabelli*

1999   Dance premiere: *Hammerklavier*

2000   Dance premieres: *Beethoven Seventh, Variations on a Theme by Haydn, Mozart Clarinet Quintet K.581,* and *Surfer at the River Styx*

2001   Dance premieres: *Known by Heart Duet, Westerly Round,* and *Hammerklavier II*

2002   Broadway: *Movin' Out*

2003   Book *The Creative Habit: Learn It and Use It for Life* is published; wins Tony Award and other theater prizes for *Movin' Out*; dance premiere: *Even the King*

2004   Receives the President's Award from the Vietnam Veterans of America; receives the National Medal of Arts; *Movin' Out* continues on Broadway while another cast takes the show on national tour

HOW TO BECOME
A DANCER OR
CHOREOGRAPHER

THE JOB

Dancers usually dance together as a chorus. As they advance in their profession, dancers may do special numbers with other selected dancers and, when a reputation is attained, the dancer may do solo work. The following are five popular forms of dancing, and although some dancers become proficient in all five, most dancers attempt to specialize in one specific area.

The *acrobatic dancer* performs a style of dancing characterized by difficult gymnastic feats.

The *ballet dancer* performs artistic dances suggesting a theme or story. Ballet is perhaps one of the most exacting and demanding forms of dance. Most other types of dancers need some type of ballet training.

The *interpretive* or *modern dancer* performs dances that interpret moods or characterizations. Facial expression and the body are used to express the theme of the dance.

The *tap dancer* performs a style of dancing that is distinguished by rhythm tapped by the feet in time with the music.

Ballroom dancers perform social dances such as the waltz, fox-trot, cha-cha, tango, and rumba.

In all dancing, grace and execution are basic. Some dances require specific traditional movements and precise positions. Others provide for planned movement but permit sufficient variation in execution. The dancer thus is able to include a spin, a dip, a pause, or some other effect that provides a certain amount of individuality and flair to the performance.

Dancing is a profession that permits the performers to make the most of their physical features and personality. Part of the success of dancers depends on the ability to use their assets in ways that will permit their full expression.

Dancers may perform in classical ballet or modern dance, in dance adaptations for musical shows, in folk dances, or in tap and other types of popular dancing productions. Some dancers compete in contests for specific types of dancing such as ballroom dancing.

Some dancers become *choreographers*, who create new ballets or dance routines. They must be knowledgeable about dancing, music, costume, lighting, and dramatics. Others are dance directors and train the dancers in productions. Many dancers combine teaching with their stage work or are full-time dance instructors in ballet schools or in colleges and universities. Some open their own dancing schools with specialties such as ballet for children or ballroom dancing.

A small number of dancers and choreographers work in music videos. While they may not become rich or famous in this line of work, it does provide good experience and increases their visibility.

REQUIREMENTS

High School

A good high school education is highly recommended for those interested in becoming dancers. You should take courses in speech, music, and dramatics, and engage in extracurricular activities that will enhance your knowledge of these areas. You should also continue your dance studies during the summer. Some summer camps feature dance training, and special summer classes are available in some large cities.

Postsecondary Training

A number of avenues for advanced training are available. About 240 colleges and universities offer programs leading to a bachelor's or higher degree in dance, generally through the departments of physical education, music, theater, or fine arts. These programs provide an opportunity for a college education and advanced preparation and training. Other possibilities include study with professional dancing teachers or attendance at a professional dance school. There are a number of such schools in the country; most of them are located in large cities.

Experience as a performer is usually required for teaching in professional schools, and graduate degrees are generally required by colleges and conservatories.

Other Requirements

There are no formal educational requirements, but an early start (around eight years old for ballet) and years of practice are basic to a successful career. The preparation for a professional dancing career is as much a test of your personal characteristics as it is of your talent. You need, first and foremost, to be enthusiastic about dancing, for the basic desire to achieve success is an ingredient that will help you overcome some of the disappointment and setbacks that seem to be hurdles normally encountered.

The physical demands of daily practice as well as the demands of the dance routine necessitate good health and a strong body. A dancer must also have a feeling for music, a sense of rhythm, and grace and agility. Good feet with normal arches are required. Persistence and sensitivity, as they apply to the day-to-day preparation of the dancer, are also important personal characteristics. Dancing is strenuous and demanding. Many dancers end their performing careers by their late thirties, although a few dancers are able to continue their careers much further. Dancers who cease to perform sometimes continue to work in the field as choreographers, company managers, or dance teachers.

EXPLORING

Dancing is a highly competitive profession, and you should take advantage of every opportunity to gain experience and increase your skills. Naturally, you should be taking dance lessons, and usually this will also give you the opportunity to perform publicly. Try to get as much experience as you can performing in public as both a solo dancer and with groups.

Your dance instructor is also a valuable source of information regarding this career. If you are interested in choreography, your instructor may allow you to work up routines to perform. Instructors can also speak from personal experience about the dance schools they attended as well as give advice about what schools they think might be right for you. If you are located near colleges or universities that offer dance programs, make an appointment to visit the department and talk to a student or faculty member there. This will increase your knowledge of what programs are available and what their requirements are.

Finally, use your library, a bookstore, or the Internet to find and read articles about dance, choreography, and happenings in the dance world. One publication to look for is *Dance Magazine* (http://www.dancemagazine.com), which contains useful information for young dancers.

EMPLOYERS

Dancers and choreographers are employed by dance companies, opera companies, theater companies, and film and video companies. They are also hired for individual shows and performances that may run anywhere from one night only to several years. Most opportunities are located in major metropolitan areas, New York City being the primary center of dance in the United States. Other cities that have full-time dance companies include San Francisco, Chicago, Boston, Philadelphia, Pittsburgh, Miami, and Washington, D.C. Many smaller cities also have their own resident dance and theater companies. After several years of experience, dancers and choreographers often start their own companies based in studios that also may offer classes to both professionals and amateurs.

Dancers and choreographers who are interested in teaching may find employment in high school and post-secondary schools. Teaching opportunities are also available in local dance studios that offer classes to age groups that vary from preschool to adult. Other employers might include local park districts, senior citizens homes, youth centers, and social service agencies like the YMCA.

STARTING OUT

The only way to get started in dancing is to dance, to take advantage of every performance opportunity possible. Local groups are usually in the market for entertainment at their meetings or social affairs. These appearances provide the opportunity to polish routines and develop the professional air that distinguishes the professional from the amateur performer. Breaking the professional barrier by achieving one's first paid performance can be accomplished in several ways. Take advantage of every audition. Follow the announcements in the trade magazines. Circulate among other dancers. Attend shows and get to know everyone who may be in a position to help with a job. Another possibility that should be considered is to register with recognized booking agents.

ADVANCEMENT

As in all performing arts, the star on the dressing room door is the dream of dancing aspirants. Yet top billing, a name in lights, or being the program headliner are positions of accomplishment reserved for a very small number. Many dancers start by earning a spot in the dancing chorus of an off-Broadway musical, in the line at a supper club, or in a dancing group on a television variety show or spectacular. Such opportunities permit further study, yet enable one to work with experienced choreographers and producers. Earning a spot as a chorus dancer in television on a regular weekly show could provide as many as 13, 26, or 39 performances with the same group.

In recent years, a number of musical stock companies have originated throughout the United States, thus providing another avenue for employment. Although many of these operate only in summer, they provide experience of a Broadway nature. Outdoor spectaculars such as exhibitions, parades, fairs, and festivals often use dance acts.

Working on the road can be an exciting, yet tiring, opportunity. Chorus groups with traveling musicals and café shows provide regular employment for a season. The numbers are rehearsed before the tour and very little adaptation or change is possible. One does get a chance to perform in a variety of situations and with different bands or orchestras because accompaniments are different in each club or community performance.

Dancers may also advance to choreographing, one of the most creative and responsible jobs in dancing. Other dancers find positions as teachers and some eventually open their own schools.

Dancers join various unions depending on the type of dance they perform. The American Guild of Musical Artists is the union to which dancers belong who perform in opera ballet, classical ballet, and modern dance. Those on live or taped television join the American Federation of Television and Radio Artists. Dancers in films have the Screen Actors Guild or the Screen Extras Guild. Those who appear onstage in musical comedies join the Actors' Equity Association. And those who dance in nightclubs and variety shows belong to the American Guild of Variety Artists.

EARNINGS

Dancers' yearly earnings vary widely depending on factors such as where a dancer is employed, how much work he or she was able to get for the year, and what role the dancer performed in a production. The U.S. Department of Labor reports that the median annual income for dancers was $21,100 in 2002. The lowest paid 10 percent of dancers earned less than $12,880 that same period, while the highest paid 10 percent made more than $53,350. Dancers on tour usually receive additional money to use for room and food and may also get extra money for overtime.

Because of the lack of steady, well-paying work, many dancers must supplement their income with earnings from other jobs. Possibilities include teaching dance, working several part-time dance jobs, or going outside the field for other work.

According to the U.S. Department of Labor, choreographers had the median yearly income of $29,470 in 2000. Like dancers' incomes, choreographers' earnings vary widely. The lowest paid 10 percent of choreographers made less than $14,000 in 2002, while at the other end of the pay scale the highest paid 10 percent earned more than $57,590.

Many dancers and choreographers belong to unions, and those working under union contracts may receive some benefits such as health insurance and paid sick leave. Those who do not work under union contracts typically receive no benefits and must provide for their own health insurance, retirement plans, and other benefits.

WORK ENVIRONMENT

The irregularity of employment is the most difficult aspect of the profession. Dancers are never certain where they will be employed or under what conditions. One may wait weeks for a contract. An offer may involve travel, night hours, or weekend rehearsals. Work on a Broadway stage show may last 20 weeks, 40 weeks, or three years, or possibly the show will fold after the third performance. With rehearsals and performances, a normal workweek runs 30 hours (six hours a day maximum).

Dancing requires considerable sacrifices of both a personal and social nature. Dancing is the performing dancer's life. The demands of practice and the need to continue lessons and to learn new routines and variations leave little time for recreational or social activities. As a career, dancing necessitates greater emphasis on self than on others; the intensive competition and the need to project oneself to get ahead leave little time for other pursuits.

OUTLOOK

Employment of dancers is expected to increase about as fast as the national occupational average through the next decade, but those seeking a career in dancing will find the field highly competitive and uncertain. For performers, there are limited opportunities since there are more trained dancers than job openings. Television has provided additional positions, but the number of stage and screen productions is declining. The best opportunities may exist in regional ballet companies, opera companies, and dance groups affiliated with colleges and universities. The turnover rate in dancing is rather high so there are always openings for the newcomer. Although generalization is difficult, the average chorus dancer can expect a career of five to 10 years at best. Most ballet dancers stop dancing for an audience before they are 40 years of age.

The dancer who can move from performing to teaching will find other employment possibilities in colleges, universities, and schools of dance; with civic and community groups; and in the operation of dance studios.

TO LEARN MORE ABOUT DANCERS AND CHOREOGRAPHERS

BOOKS

Franklin, Eric. *Conditioning for Dance.* Champaign, Ill.: Human Kinetics, 2003.

———. *Dance Imagery for Technique and Performance.* Champaign, Ill.: Human Kinetics, 1997.

Freedman, Russell. *Martha Graham: A Dancer's Life.* New York: Clarion Books, 1998.

Grant, Gail. *Technical Manual and Dictionary of Classical Ballet.* 3d ed. Mineola, N.Y.: Dover, 1967.

Reynolds, Nancy, and Malcolm McCormick. *No Fixed Points: Dance in the Twentieth Century.* New Haven, Conn.: Yale University Press, 2003.

ORGANIZATIONS AND WEBSITES

This is a union for singers, dancers, and other performers in operas and other classical music productions and concerts. The website has information on auditions, legal actions against employers, and union news.

American Guild of Musical Artists

1430 Broadway, 14th Floor

New York, NY 10018-3308

Tel: 212-265-3687

Email: AGMA@MusicalArtists.org

http://www.musicalartists.org

Visit *Dance Magazine's* website to read abstracts of articles that appear in the print version. For general questions, contact

Dance Magazine

333 Seventh Avenue, 11th Floor

New York, NY 10001-5004

Tel: 212-979-4803

Email: dancemag@dancemagazine.com

http://www.dancemagazine.com

A directory of dance companies and related organizations and other information on professional dance is available from Dance/USA. Visit the Young Dancer

Information link on its website for helpful news and advice.

Dance/USA

1156 15th Street, NW, Suite 820

Washington, DC 20005-1726

Tel: 202-833-1717

Email: danceusa@danceusa.org

http://www.danceusa.org

A directory of accredited programs is available from NASD. Approved member institutions can also be found listed on its website, which also contains a helpful FAQ section for students.

National Association of Schools of Dance (NASD)

11250 Roger Beacon Drive, Suite 21

Reston, VA 20190-5219

Tel: 703-437-0700

Email: info@arts-accredit.org

http://nasd.arts-accredit.org

NDA compiles a dance directory with information on universities, colleges, dance studios, and high schools that offer dance education and programs. Visit its website for more information on the directory and scholarships and awards.

National Dance Association (NDA)

American Alliance for Health, Physical Education,
Recreation & Dance
1900 Association Drive
Reston, VA 20191-1598
Tel: 800-213-7193
E-mail: nda@aahperd.org
www.aahperd.org/nda

TO LEARN MORE ABOUT TWYLA THARP

BOOKS

Bremser, Martha. *Fifty Contemporary Choreographers*. New York: Routledge, 1999.

Byers, Paula K., ed. *Encyclopedia of World Biography*. Detroit: Gale Research, 1998.

Coe, Robert. *Dance in America*. New York: E. P. Dutton, 1985.

Editors. *Current Biography Yearbook 1975*. New York: H. W. Wilson, 1976.

Jonas, Gerald. *Dancing: The Pleasure, Power, and Art of Movement*. New York: Harry Abrams, 1992.

Mazo, Joseph. *Prime Movers: The Makers of Modern Dance in America.* 2nd ed. Chicago: Independent Publishers Group, 2000.

Mooney, Louise, ed. *Newsmakers: The People Behind Today's Headlines*. Detroit: Gale Research, 1992.

Reynolds, Nancy, and Malcolm McCormick. *No Fixed Points: Dance in the Twentieth Century*. New Haven, Conn.: Yale University Press, 2003.

Riggs, Thomas, ed. *Contemporary, Theatre, Film and Television, Vol. 51*. Detroit: Thomson Gale, 2003.

Rogosin, Elinor. *The Dance Makers: Conversations with American Choreographers*. New York: Walker and Co., 1980.

Tharp, Twyla. *The Creative Habit: Learn It and Use It for Life*. New York: Simon & Schuster, 2003.

———. *Push Comes to Shove*. New York: Bantam, 1992.

WEBSITES

Academy of Achievement

http://www.achievement.org

American Ballet Theatre

http://www.abt.org

E! Online

http:// www.eonline.com

Internet Movie Database

http://www.imdb.com

Internet Theater Database

http://www.achievement.org

Theatermania

http://www.theatermania.com

Twyla Tharp Dance

http://www.twylatharp.org

INDEX

Page numbers in *italics* indicate illustrations.

ABOUT THE AUTHOR

James Robert Parish, a former entertainment reporter, publicist, and book series editor, is the author of numerous biographies and reference books of the entertainment industry including *Denzel Washington: Actor, Halle Berry: Actor, Stephen King: Writer, Tom Hanks: Actor, Steven Spielberg: Filmmaker, Whitney Houston, The Hollywood Book of Love, Hollywood Divas, Hollywood Bad Boys, The Encyclopedia of Ethnic Groups in Hollywood, Jet Li, Jason Biggs, Gus Van Sant, The Hollywood Book of Death, Whoopi Goldberg, Rosie O'Donnell's Story, The Unofficial "Murder, She Wrote" Casebook, Today's Black Hollywood, Let's Talk! America's Favorite TV Talk Show Hosts, The Great Cop Pictures, Liza Minnelli, The Elvis Presley Scrapbook, Jeanette MacDonald,* and *Hollywood's Great Love Teams.*

Mr. Parish is a frequent on-camera interviewee on cable and network TV for documentaries on the performing arts both in the United States and in the United Kingdom. He resides in Studio City, California.